Praise for *Great Little Editing Tips for Writers*

This "great little book" of editing tips gives readers a down-to-earth and refreshing approach to better grammar and usage. Grammarians bemoan the incorrect wording of the sign "ten items or less" and chuckle over a sign advertising "tattoo's." (Whose tattoo, exactly?) While we are imperfect writers living in an imperfect world filled with grammar mistakes and mispronunciations, it's editing books like this that helps us get one step closer to writing and speaking, clearly and succinctly.
~ DAWN COLCLASURE, author, *365 Tips for Writers: Inspiration, Writing Prompts and Beat the Block Tips...*

Words such as *climactic* and *climatic* used improperly or misspelled can mean a rejection when submitting to the "gatekeepers." The addition or deletion of that little second "c" makes a huge difference in the meaning of the word. I happen to be a fan of Carolyn Howard-Johnson's Frugal series, they are a part of my writing and marketing toolkit. I learned a great deal from *Great Little Last-Minute Editing Tips for Writers* and will be referring to it often; I highly recommend it.
~ KAREN CIOFFI, author, writer-for-hire, freelance writer

The best way to appear amateurish as writers is to make simple word usage errors. Writers should know the difference between these homophone words and know which of them to use in their copy. Author and editor Carolyn Howard-Johnson lists some of the most common errors in *Great Little Last-Minute Editing Tips for Writers*. This reviewer found this pamphlet to be inspirational and a brush up for any writer. Any time a writer submits copy not up to professional standards there is a gatekeeper who will bounce it. Reading this reference guide can save writers the embarrassment of receiving a rejection slip for poor writing.
~ ROBERT MEDAK, reviewer, *New York Journal of Books*

Carolyn Howard-Johnson is well known among writers for her helpful book *The Frugal Book Promoter*, and she continues to encourage and guide writers through her many other projects, including this fast read (50+ pages). The meat of the book is page after page of handy references for spotting and fixing tricky word pairs. Organized alphabetically with word pairs separated by slashes (e.g., "bereft / bereaved"), the book makes it easy to look up definitions and identify which word should be used in specific circumstances. Priced reasonably (especially the Kindle version) and packed with lots of writerly wit and humor, the book makes for both an enjoyable read and a worthwhile reference.
~ K.M. WEILAND author, *Structuring Your Novel* and *Creating Character Arcs*

This is a wonderful book that could be used as a reference book in secondary classrooms and writing groups. The author explains the zero tolerance policy of writing contest judges for word-use errors. Be informed and advised with this book when proofing for yourself and others. The book would also be handy during teacher-student writing conferences as a neutral way to discuss word use errors especially.
~ CAROLYN WILHELM, curriculum writer, *The Wise Owl Factory*

Carolyn Howard-Johnson delivers a succinct, easy to follow guide that really does take you by the hand and help you over the editing hurdles. You will bypass the "Gatekeepers" if you follow her directions. Whether you plan to self-publish or seek a traditional publisher, you will need to make sure your prose is as good as it can be and this little guide will certainly put you ahead of the pack. I highly recommend any of Carolyn Howard-Johnson's books and this is no exception. Go get it now! You won't be sorry.
~ BILLIE A. WILLIAMS, author, *Writing Wider, More Exercises in Creative Writing: A Creative Writers Mentor*

Carolyn Howard-Johnson's booklet *Great Little Last-Minute Editing Tips for Writers* is a wonderful resource for all writers and editors. It is actually an addendum to her book *The Frugal Editor: Put Your Best Book Forward to Avoid Humiliation and Ensure Success*. As a writer and editor, I see this booklet as something that I will keep very handy. It seems that no matter how many times I research some words, they just won't stick in this head of mine. This book is set up as a small dictionary of often-confused words and makes them easy to find. Warning: If readers come across this book first, they will most likely find themselves ordering *The Frugal Editor*. That is what I did, and I wasn't disappointed. Both books are excellent writing reference tools.

~ JOYCE M. GILMOUR, proprietor, *Editing TLC*

Great Little Last-Minute Editing Tips for Writers was an easy read and done in one sitting. Another stroke of brilliance. Who would have the time to read, cover-to-cover, a 300-page book of word-use? However, I'm holding back some final praise unless you guarantee me there will be other books like this to follow. Yes? I mean, what about the words, "title—entitled?" Or "affect—effect?" I can go on. They don't call me a *gabologist* for nothing. Do me and the rest of the literary world a favor. Get back to the keyboard and crank them out. Of course they're not for *meeee*, they're for a friend. Ahem.

~ GEORGIA RICHARDSON, author, *A Funny Thing Happened on the Way to the Throne*

Carolyn Howard-Johnson's *new Great Little Last-Minute Editing Tips for Writers* is subtitled *The Ultimate Frugal Booklet for Avoiding Word Trippers and Crafting Gatekeeper-Perfect Copy*, and with good reason. If you or someone you know went through school fighting the English language—cannot spell, were not taught grammar, or simply struggle with the English language and its propensity for homonyms—this is a book that should LIVE on your desk, in your notebook, or next to your computer. Whether you write in coffee shops, on the beach, or catalog notes on your smart phone, there will come a time to make your draft letter-perfect. When it's time to finalize a job application, a query letter or a manuscript submission, refer to *Great Little Last-Minute Editing Tips*. The basics such as "altogether" vs. "all together" to the arcane, "karat" vs. "carat" appear in clear explanations. Howard-Johnson keeps the lessons light with personal anecdotes and strong examples. Skip your spell-checker except for typos and buy this book for the knowledge of what is the what. Or is it what is the which? Regardless, (no *irregardless*, please!), write with confidence and enjoy.

~ EILEEN GRANFORS, author, *The Marisol Trilogy*

A successful author, editor, writing and publishing consultant, Carolyn Howard-Johnson draws upon her many years of experience and expertise to compile a brief compendium of user friendly and immanently practical advice that will enable writers to avoid commonly encountered errors of spelling and thereby making their work, be it a blog, a letter, or the next Great American Novel, to be all that it should. This book is highly recommended reading for anyone preparing to write pretty much anything—and a fascinating read in its own right for those who appreciate wordplay and the occasionally encountered dilemmas of the English language!

~ JIM COX, Editor-in-Chief, *Midwest Book Review*

This gem of a book proves that good things can come in small packages. Small enough to carry around in your writing folder, full of enough useful and entertaining content to be much heftier, this book on word trippers is a valuable reference that will keep you out of jail. Well, not jail, but at least out of the doghouse when writers submit queries and manuscripts. *Word trippers* is a great term for these little gremlins that occasionally confound even the best of us and routinely trip up the careless. Most writers are acutely aware of the distinction between *anxious* and *eager* (though it's not clear that TV script writers are). But how about *bereft* and *bereaved*? Some distinctions are quite subtle (*capability* vs. *ability*), others more obvious (*dissent* vs. *descent*). Carolyn skillfully explains the differences and provides practical examples.

~ C. SUTTON, Amazon Reviewer

Great Little Last-Minute Editing Tips for Writers

(Second Edition)

The Ultimate Frugal Reference Guide
for Avoiding Word Trippers and
Crafting Gatekeeper-Perfect Copy

By Carolyn Howard-Johnson

Modern History Press
Ann Arbor, MI

Great Little Last-Minute Editing Tips for Writers: The Ultimate Frugal Reference Guide for Avoiding Word Trippers and Crafting Gatekeeper-Perfect Copy, 2nd Edition

ISBN 978-1-61599-524-0 paperback
ISBN 978-1-61599-525-7 hardcover
ISBN 978-1-61599-526-4 eBook

Modern History Press   Tollfree 888-761-6268
5145 Pontiac Trail   FAX 734-663-6861
Ann Arbor, MI 48105   info@ModernHistoryPress.com
Cover design by Victor Volkman

Dedicated to Trudy McMurrin, editor extraordinaire, whose editing skills live on through the books she edited and the many authors she mentored.

Contents

Acknowledgments

Other than the usual stylebooks, dictionaries, thesauri and other reference materials one uses to write a reference guide like this, my special thanks go to June Casagrande. We were both freelance writers for the *Glendale News-Press* where she writes a weekly column on grammar called "A Word, Please," but we had never met. Then she enrolled in the Writers' Program class I taught at UCLA and we became good friends. I read her columns avidly and they never fail to give me new ideas.

Thanks and much love also go to Trudy McMurrin who died too early of breast cancer after she edited *The Frugal Editor: Put Your Best Book Forward to Avoid Humiliation,* second in my HowToDoItFrugally Series of books for writers. With more than three decades of university press editing experience and nearly as many as a freelance editor, she was not only responsible for keeping me viewing my own copy with clarity but was a constant source of new grammar tidbits.

In Trudy's absence, Nadine Laman of Cactus Rain Publishing and Yvonne Perry of Writers in the Sky fame stepped in as last-minute saviors. How does that song go? "With a little help from our friends?"

And now Victor Volkman, publisher at Modern History Press, a division of Loving Healing Press, has offered to publisher this reference guide in its second edition. With additions and updates, of course. It seems gratitude is indeed part of the joy of writing and helper-books like this are one way for me to spread that joy through the writing community.

Before You Get Started

This reference guide is an addendum to a list of word trippers and other gremlins that plague writers in the appendix of my book, *The Frugal Editor: Put Your Best Book Forward to Avoid Humiliation and Ensure Success*. A short work like this cannot accommodate the huge list of word trippers. The English language is so complex we could fill volumes with similar nemeses to writers and editors alike. I hoped to have many more quick studies for you. So far, an update—second edition—seems to be the next best step.

My earlier book, *The Frugal Editor*, includes a list of the most frequent word trippers and other booboos I encounter as an editor of others' manuscripts. My intent was to give writers as many tips as I could in easily absorbed increments, tips that will advance their editing craft. And that craft is as essential to writers as their writing skills—even when they are fortunate enough to be assigned a talented editor or flush enough to hire the best for themselves. Trouble is, the list needed to be longer and the book needed to be smaller for those who haven't yet taken to Kindle or other readers.

Thus *Great Little Last-Minute Tips for Writers* was born. Now in its second edition from Modern History Press, it is full of words that are trouble causers—all of them different from the ones in *The Frugal Editor*. Specifically, they either sound alike or are spelled similarly. They are not arcane words that you will seldom have an occasion to use. They are not words the writer knows but still mistypes. Words like *to/too/two* and *their/there/they're*. We've known about those guys and their kin since third grade. Misusing them is a case of your brain and fingers going a bit haywire as you write. Certainly their misuse has nothing to do with your knowing their sneaky ways, and there's no help for their confusion other than, as *The Frugal Editor* suggests, hiring a second pair of eyes or reading final manuscripts backwards. Even effective computer tools like Microsoft Word's Spell Checker won't help. These are little things you just gotta *know*.

What I have added for this second edition is more about the ever-tense relationship between grammar rules and style choices. The famous *Elements of Style* was never intended as a grammar book; it was a very useful guide of Strunk et al's preferences for his students. It is unfortunate that many students (and writers!) treated it as if everything he preferred were rules chiseled in stone. Honestly, my mini-treatise on *style choice* is the part of this reference guide I think most important. So, please keep reading even if you are already a whiz at homonyms. (Please note that in the Appendix of this book I have recommended an updated edition of Strunk and a few other references that treat grammar rules, structure, and other "elements of style" as the choices that they are!).

It is my hope that—because the paper version of this reference guide is slim—writers might take it with them to read and refresh when they are on the go. Better yet, get the Kindle version and have it always available on your tablet, eReader, and laptop. I also wanted to keep it short so they won't be daunted by too much to learn. I mean, who wants to tackle the Associated Press or Chicago Manual stylebooks in one sitting!

The English language is groping toward a million words. Compared to many other languages, that is a huge number. I won't tell you how many French has, as an example, because it's a touchy subject and experts disagree anyway. French word-watchers discourage diluting (polluting?) their language with foreign words so the heft of their dictionary is noticeably light.

In addition, language evolves. Those of us who went to school back in the dark ages must adapt. Younger readers may wonder what all the fuss is about, but even you young ones will have to adapt to future changes. The computerized world is moving along at a faster clip than ever before and contributing to changes at the same rate.

The point is that it is no wonder those who write in English—those who love words, have studied words, or have a natural facility for words—will always have more to learn. I think we mere mortal writers should strive to learn enough about editing that we'll pick up on errors our editors overlook. I've actually *seen* editors overlook the *childlike/childish* entry in this reference guide.

Before I sign off, I want to make it clear that I believe one's voice should come through in all kinds of writing, including texts. The reader should get a sense of who the author is, even in books on grammar. That means I get to talk to you as if we were chatting at Starbucks. And I'm cautioning you, you don't want an editor to clean up language that makes the personal you come through. For a longer discussion on what to expect from an editor, please refer to *The Frugal Editor,* the second book in this series.

After the word trippers, I include a list of books for further study, including the ones I mentioned above. I hope you'll read more than one.

Mark Twain knew the importance of making the correct word choice. He said, "The difference between the right word and the almost-right word is the difference between lightning and the lightning bug."

Okay, let's get started on trip-you-up words and on giving you the courage to feel strong about making a style choice.

Pleasing the Gatekeepers

This very brief section is a bit of a disclaimer for those whose path to publishing includes pleasing gatekeepers, whoever they might be. They differ from medium to medium and industry to industry. You may want to be "right," but when "right" may be misunderstood or feel odd to your audience, it may be better to avoid the situation by finding another word by using a good thesaurus or changing the way you construct your sentence. Writing, after all, is about communication. When you work around a situation like this, you are not making a choice between "right" and "wrong," but about doing the job you set out to do when you put pen to paper or started typing.

Where You Get to Choose

The section before this brings us smack-dab to "style choice," a choice that rule-oriented sticklers may be averse to or didn't know existed because they are so firmly entrenched in what I call the "comma syndrome." These poor souls have taught there is only one way to attack anything to do with language be it spelling, grammar rules, syntax, or whatever. They keep searching for a clear set of rules about how to use commas that apply in every instance and end up letting Spell Checker put commas anywhere it wants to and are likely to suffer from dreaded ailments like writers' block, an irrational fear-of-editors' suggestions or the belief that they must always accept what an editor suggests or, worse, won't accept what they suggest in any case because...well, how could an expert who makes their living doing something know anything different from the rules the author learned in the fourth grade and still be "right."

If you are in the midst of a first project writing fiction or dialogue you may have already experienced conflicts. Are you really expected to write poor grammar if you are writing dialogue for a character who talks that way? Expected? No. But you'll make better choices if you know you can, know that it's "right" or at least "okay" to do so. What about poetry? Can you make up your own words. Did you read the poem "Jabberwocky" by Lewis Carroll when you were a kid. I'll refresh your memory with the opening stanzas:

> 'Twas brillig, and the slithy toves
>   Did gyre and gimble in the wabe:
> All mimsy were the borogoves,
>   And the mome raths outgrabe.
>
> "Beware the Jabberwock, my son!
>   The jaws that bite, the claws that catch!
> Beware the Jubjub bird, and shun
>   The frumious Bandersnatch!"

The trick is to keep an open mind about language. It fluctuates endlessly, anyway. It's a beautiful, growing thing that sets us apart from other lifeforms and brings us closer to the things in life that we love. Choice is a beautiful thing. Do your research. Know more tomorrow than you do today. And have fun with it!

Trip-You-Up Words

adapting / adopting: These are good words to start with because it's often words that aren't homonyms but differ by only one letter that give us trouble. When we type them wrong, they're hard to spot. This is your reminder to watch these two and others that are similar. Pay even more attention to them when you know their meanings. And watch your autocorrect feature because it often guesses wrong as you type.

adverse / averse: Some of the words in this reference guide trip us up because we're rarely warned about them, because we may hear them wrong in our minds, or our minds make our ears hear what it thinks they should hear. It's also because we are rarely put on the alert about them. We are not *adverse* to an idea, we are *averse* to it. We are opposed to it. Even though the two words come from the same root and are similar in meaning, *adverse* means that something is harmful or has a negative connotation. So we may be *averse* to doing something because it presents *adverse* conditions. *Adverse* describes the condition of something. *Averse* is more about how we feel about it.

advice / advise: I sometimes think the misuse of these words has more to do with thoughtless typing than with misunderstanding their uses. But not always. *Advice* is a noun. *Advise* is a verb. Here's an example: "I sensed she wanted me to *advise* her, so I gave her this astute *advice*: 'Drop the guy.'"

aesthetic / esthetic: Most experts agree that *esthetic* is a "variable of aesthetic." According to Webster, *esthetic* has to do with mere sensation. *Aesthetic* is closer to the original Greek and connotes a meaning more closely related to beauty or sensitivity to art. It is also more commonly used in both the

US and Britain. The two are so closely related it seems foolish to stray from *aesthetic* when it may give you extra points in a gatekeeper's subconscious rating system.

all tolled / all told: You and I both might think *told* and then start thinking again—thinking too hard—and decide on *tolled*. This is one of those places where our instincts work better. It is *told*. Go for it!

although / though: These two words are pretty much interchangeable. *Although*, is a bit more formal. Having said that, if you're working on my zero-tolerance rule for getting your submissions past the nit-pickiest of gatekeepers in the publishing industry, use *although* in your cover letters, queries and proposals when either feel comfortable. *Though*, by itself means "contingent upon," and its importance has become evident by a recent impeachment trial. We may never have thought about it before, but since then its use may conjure up something you didn't intend

> Notice to those learning English as a second language: Do not use either of these words when *in spite of* or *despite* are preferable. See the *despite* or *in spite of* entry.

all together / altogether: The Germanic habit of pushing two words into one word often gives English speakers fits, especially when English sometimes uses them as two words. To decide which to use, we need to think about their meaning and how they are functioning in the sentence. *Altogether* is an adverb that means entirely. Things are *altogether* too long, too difficult, too boring. *All together* specifically refers to a group. "We are going all together." Test this by putting the verb between the *all* and the *together*. We can *all* play *together*. We can *all* go *together*. We can *all* travel *together*. When you can juggle the words like this and make them sound right, you can unjumble them back to *play all together, go all together, travel all together*. After you have finished your decision-making process, you might prefer to *use* the sequencing I just recommended as a test—that is put the verb *between* the all and together. Between being the operative word here. I somehow nearly always like it better.

among / amongst: Style guides and dictionaries tend to disagree on this one. Here's your zero-tolerance rule for American English. Skip *amongst* altogether. You other English-speakers? Have at it.

anxious / eager: You're *eager* to learn new things. You get *anxious* when a friend coaxes you into going for your first parachute jump. Big difference. You can find style guides that tell you to use them any old way you want, but it's not wise when the gatekeepers are looking.

auger / augur: Rarely will you (or your editor) need this. But when the occasion arises and you know it, you'll be considered really, really good at what you do. *Auger* is a hole-piercing tool. *Augur* is to predict.

author / writer: To say, "He authors a book" may not be wrong. In English we get to make nouns into verbs if we insist. Do it with *author* in your query letter and you may irritate the agent you're trying to impress. It feels strained as if one is trying too hard to be well—authorly. Use the plain old verb *to write*. "He *wrote* a book titled…" While we're talking about agent-averse choices, please don't "pen" something when you "write" it. Everyone will suspect you are trying too hard.

bereft / bereaved: Easy. *Bereft* is a general feeling of sadness. *Bereaved* is sorrow caused by concern over another's death.

bi- / semi-: As we were growing up, we used these prefixes inter-changeably. Now we're writers we'll use *bi* when we mean every other year or two-of-any unit intervals. *Semi* means two times in any given period of time. So a newsletter that goes out twice a month is a *semimonthly* newsletter. If it is issued every other month, *bimonthly* is the word we want to use.

borne / born: Usually writers will type in *born* without thinking. But if the intent is to use past tense form of the verb *to bear,* use *borne.* "That he was *born* a Scorpio is a weight she has *borne* on her shoulders her entire life."

bring / take: These words are often misused, both in print and in speech. Your choice is dictated by the direction of the action. Is it coming toward or going away from the subject noun of the sentence? Use *bring* when the object is being brought toward the subject. Use *take* when the item is being taken away from it. You do not "*bring* potatoes to the old woman who lives in Calavaras County," you *take* them to her. But you "*brought* them with you" when you took them to her.

capability / ability: *Ability* is related to the word *able.* To be able to do something requires skill. *Capability* has a sense of possibility to it. She has the *ability* necessary to write clearly but doesn't have the *capability* to think or write with imagery.

carat / karat: The pros use *carat* to indicate the weight of diamonds and other precious stones. However, *karat* with a *k* measures the percentage of pure gold that is present in jewelry. It is often abbreviated to become 18 K or 14 K.

canvas / canvass: Here is one you know if you are writing copy for a candidate's run for political office. *Canvas* is a heavy tarp-like cloth. It may be large enough to cover your garage or small enough for an artist who paints in oils to stretch over wooden bars as a base for her paint. *Canvass* is to cover an area to solicit votes or opinions or to look for missing children.

censor / censure: Writers usually aren't keen on being *censored* so knowing the difference may be especially important to them. *Censor* is a verb that means using a set of values—values that may or may not agree with a writer's—to accept or delete his or her material. *Censure* means to reprimand or blame. As a writer you would probably want to *censure* a person who *censored* the political beliefs you expressed in your essay. In other words, you would tell him—in no uncertain terms—how much you disapprove.

childlike / childish: I see these words misused all the time. Worse, when we error, the mistake is often missed by editors. *Childlike* is used to describe the qualities of being a child that we'd rather not lose. A sense of wonder, perhaps. *Childish* is an adjective use derogatorily to mean immature.

climactic / climatic: The former refers to a climax—of your short story, perhaps; the second is all about the weather.

comment / commentary: When you visit a blog, you may *comment* on the post. That's your brief statement or opinion. *Commentary* is much longer. The sidekick baseball announcers are big on commentary. My gawd! Those statistics and opinions! They go on *ad infinitum*.

couldn't care less / could care less: If you mean that you really don't give a darn about something you say, "I *couldn't care less* about that measly problem." It means there is no way you could care any less about something. When you use the other term, you are really saying that you *could* care more. Trouble is, if you use it that way, you will probably be misunderstood because it is misused so often. Use it wrong and you'll have editors thinking you are guilty of fuzzy thinking. Because we're interested in clearer English, it may be best to steer clear of it altogether.

counsel / council: *Counsel* is the verb for giving advice, though this spelling is also used for lawyers because they do just that. *Council* is a noun for a group of people who come together to make decisions, like a city council.

despite / in spite of / although: Grammar and style guru Bryan Garner, says *despite* and *in spite of* are interchangeable. He also believes the "compactness of *despite* recommends it." I'd interpret that to mean, no point in getting in a fuss about it, but in the interest of avoiding wordiness, use *despite*. People who speak English as a second language sometimes have trouble with this meaning. Please see the *although* entry.

demur / demure: A debutante may be *demure*. *Demure* is an adjective for modest, perhaps a bit naive. *Demur* is a verb that means to voice opposition or to delay a decision or action.

display: I found this little warning in David Pogue's *New York Times* column. He occasionally rants about the use of jargon. I can't say it better, so here it is: "'Display' can be a noun ('a display of fireworks'). It can also be a verb that takes a direct object ('He displayed emotion.'). It is not, however, a verb without a direct object, except in magazines like *PC World*: 'Shows filmed in high-definition end up displaying in letterbox format.'" Displaying what in letterbox format? Fireworks? Emotions? The word this writer was looking for is 'appearing.'" See what I mean by picky editors? They see. They know. They get peeved. Even if you don't have a fuss budget checking your copy, you *do* care about better English or you wouldn't be reading this reference guide. Even those who write how-to manuals aren't *required* to replace words that have been working well for centuries with ugly jargon.

dissent / descent: This is one of those errors that gets made even when people know the difference. Once made, it seems as if few can ferret it out of their copy. I've seen it used incorrectly in books printed by the finest publishers. You know the difference, so if you watch for it you can make the right choice. *Dissent* is to differ in opinion. A trick for remembering: *Descent* is related to *descend* or "go down."

diffuse / defuse: Some words are seldom seen in print, at least not together. And they sound so similar we may not separate them in that figurative dictionary we carry around in our heads. We *defuse* bombs and conflict. *Diffuse* means to spread something and, by extension, to spread it more thinly.

disperse / disburse: This is another tricky one we're rarely warned about (see the entry above). *Disperse* means to scatter and *disburse* means to give or pay out money, usually very carefully and not in a shotgun fashion.

distress / duress: *Distress* means pain, sorrow, or anxiety. *Duress* is about what we feel when we are under forced restraint or coercion.

emotional: *Reader's Digest* has a feature called "Toward Better English." Anyone interested in that topic should avoid using *emotional* to describe something that can have no emotions. Reporters on the scene of an accident often incorrectly describe the scene as *emotional.* That attributes a feeling to something that can't have feeling. Its use deprives a writer of describing a situation more effectively. If you see it in your copy, examine it with an eye to "Better English." There are times personification can be used to good effect. You'll know the difference when you see it.

enable: Watch the word *enable.* No one says "enable the TV function" and you shouldn't either. We see it all the time in instruction manuals, though. Really. On occasions like this, "Turn it on," will do just fine, thank you.

every day / everyday: *Everyday* is an adjective that precedes a noun. "It is an *everyday* occurrence." So when we say, "I write *every day,*" the words are separated. I see *everyday* used incorrectly every single day. Probably because our Spell Checkers do not alert us to its misuse.

fact / factoid: Factoid means the opposite of fact. It is a piece of information that is presented in the media (or elsewhere, perhaps?) as a fact but, in fact, is false. That so many people misuse it as a cute synonym for fact doesn't make it right, though some say those who use *factoid* incorrectly may win the fact/factoid battle. When that happens, we will have lost a useful word (*factoid*) for which English has no viable replacement. A similar process is happening with the misuse of the word "peruse." This process always obscures the clarity of our communication because we must try to guess depending on context. (See below for the correct use of the word *perused*.)

feat / feet: The confusion on this one is hardly worth mentioning except that you'd be surprised at how many times I see brain freeze take over editors who know the difference between the amazing *feat* of endurance required to write a novel and sore *feet*.

fissures / fishers: It's my theory that words we don't use or see often paired with words we see frequently give us trouble. Our brains just don't pause long enough for us to get that Aha! moment. *Fissures* are deep cracks. *Fishers* are those who fish.

further / farther: For most this is merely a refresher but those who research their use may notice that a few style books (the minority) claim that the distinction between the words *further* and *farther* has become blurred. True, but most gatekeepers are people who know the niceties of English. In fact, they tend to *love* the subtleties. In your effort to look like a professional, use *farther* for distances that could be measured with a ruler or any other device and *further* for figurative uses related to time or space.

gage / gauge: Merriam-Webster doesn't list *gage* as a verb. Period. It says the noun *gage* refers to something that writers rarely have an occasion to use. *Gage* is a "token of defiance" as used in the Middle Ages when people cast upon the ground a glove as a pledge to combat. When you need a verb meaning *to measure*—or a noun for a gadget that measures something, stick with *gauge*.

hare / hair: This is one that we usually get right except in *harebrained*. After all, both *hare* and *hair* can be small, insignificant. "*Hair*brained" seems about right. Lucky us. Microsoft Word will give us that angry red squiggle unless some *hare*brained editor has told you to turn off your Spell Checker.

have got / have gotten: As a past tense form of *get*, *have got* is preferred in Britain, *have gotten* is preferred in the USA. For our zero-tolerance stance to get by gatekeepers, it's best not to use *have got* as a substitute for plain old *have*. The former is not preferred by most sources, though it's not exactly wrong. "Wordy!" sniff the sticklers. And a bit strained as well.

hope / hopefully: We are often told we should never say "Hopefully, I won't have to do that," and we're still getting it wrong. We might find it easier to remember if we were told what to do rather than what not to do. Instead of saying "Hopefully, he'll help me edit this," just say, "I hope he'll help me edit this." You'll avoid lots of eye rolling and your intent will be clearer, too. (Using *hopefully* the other way is considered acceptable by some style books. In zero-tolerance mode, *acceptable* feels like a dangerous judgement.)

imply / infer: Occasionally you want to *imply* something rather than say it directly. Your listener is left to *infer* what you meant. These words are all about the communicator and the communicatee. No, *communicatee* is not an official word but it helps make the difference between the two words clear. In English, we get to make up a word now and then as long as we don't do it at the threshold of a gatekeeper.

intense / intensive: They both mean extreme. So what's the big deal? *Intensive* is imposed from without, *intense* from within. It's *intensive* care and *intense* feeling.

irritate / aggravate: To *aggravate* someone or something is to escalate or worsen a situation or the feelings of a person. I can't think of an instance in which you would *irritate* a situation or an inanimate object. You might, however, turn the sentence around and say "I find the situation irritating" but it's easier to remember (and more zero-tolerance friendly) to remember that when a person is involved in ways beyond the sensitivity of her skin, use *aggravate*.

It is what it is.: Did this sentence get popular because it is so handy when we want to obfuscate or we haven't a clue how to clarify? Avoid it except, perhaps, in dialogue coming from the mouth of a character who is likely to say useless things, use clichés, or otherwise lacks respect for the English language.

i.e. / e.g.: When you want to use *e.g.*, check to see if you mean *for example*. "The book tour took us to many cities, e.g., Phoenix, Pasadena, and Seattle. Using *i.e.* helps you clarify a point. "He is an existentialist, i.e., he believes that...." If you can substitute the words *that is* or *in other words* for the i.e., you probably have it right. Also notice that generally these initials are set off by commas on either side. We tend to pause both before and after their use.

lightening / lightning: Here's an easy one for an editor to overlook. *Lightning* is the companion to thunder. *Lightening* is usually a verb (though, thanks to the flexibility of the English language it can appear as a noun). It means to make lighter in color or, occasionally, makes it lighter in weight.

lose / loose: Everyone knows the difference between these two but it's still in the top-ten one-word edits I make for my clients. Perhaps they get confused. Perhaps the gremlins (the ones I introduced to you in *The Frugal Editor*) are at work. *Lose* is the present tense of the verb *lose/lost/lost*. *Loose* is an adjective and, sometimes, an adverb. Substitute the word *slack* as a test to see if you should use the word *loose*.

to lie / to lay: These are two different verbs. I could write an entire booklet on this subject alone. It takes but a paragraph for those familiar with the parts of speech so give it a try: The verb *to lie* does *not* take a direct object. The verb *to lay* does. So if there is a direct object in your sentence, use *lay/laid /laid*. Problems arise because the past tense of *to lie* is the same as the present tense of *to lay* and because almost everyone uses the verb *to lie* incorrectly in casual conversation. If the direct object rule doesn't help, maybe this will. You *lie* out in the sun to get a tan (no direct object). If the action is in the past, you say, "Yesterday I *lay* out in the sun." You tell your dog, "*Lie* down, Fido." With a helping verb it's "I have *lain...*" For most, those feel comfortable enough, but most everybody feels self conscious saying *have, has,* or *had lain*. So work around it. When you must use that tense, try another verb, rearrange the structure of your sentence, or use another handy tool like simile or metaphor to get your meaning across.

loathe / loath: *Loathe* means to hate beyond comparison. *Loath* (without the e) means reluctant. The *th* sounds in these two words are pronounced slightly differently and that can help you tell the difference. Notice the difference in their lisps when you say: "I am *loath* to weigh in on some usage because everyone already knows it and I *loathe* weighing in on others because there is always someone who will think I'm wrong." It may be impossible to tease out the real meaning from context if it is spelled incorrectly.

manner / manor: *Manor* is a district or area presided over by a lord in medieval times. It has come to mean the large home that was on that land. *Manner* is the way things happen or are done—for better or worse.

masterly / masterful: *Masterful* means domineering or overpowering. *Masterly* is about having a highly developed talent.

mischievious: Hey! Just take out the third "*i*" and use *mischievous* instead. Not to worry. If your word processor's spell and grammar check is on, it will alert you with a red squiggle or even autocorrect it to *mischievous* for you.

moral / morale: Because they are both nouns, these words tend to cause trouble. *Moral* is a noun often used by writers as in "the moral of a story," but also means ethical or religious practices or teachings and that does get very close to *morale*. Use *morale* for emotional attitudes or *esprit de corps*. If you say them out loud in the context of your sentence, it will help.

nauseous / nauseating / nauseated: *Strunk and White* says *nauseous* means only "sickening to contemplate." Example: The smell of artichokes is nauseous. You are *nauseated* when you feel sick to your stomach when you smell them. Many other stylebooks have dropped the distinction because these words were misused for so long and because so many people think that if the smell of artichokes is *nauseous*, they are, then, *nauseating*. Something like 82% of people don't make the distinction according to the *American Heritage® Book of English Usage*. What happens if your gatekeeper is a *Strunk and White* fan? What if he or she is over fifty and a stickler? I believe in adhering to Strunk's suggestion when submitting material to gatekeepers. I also believe we should keep an open mind when we see these words used interchangeably elsewhere, otherwise we might become nauseated.

nonchalant: Contrary to popular belief, *nonchalant* doesn't mean *casual*. It means disregarding something. There are times when this adjective applies in both cases, but when you only mean casual, use *casual* or your thesaurus. The word *nonchalant* might also mean unconcerned about drawing attention to oneself (related to *casual* in an odd kind of way) or having a confident demeanor. Yes, I know some stylebooks will tell you that you can use the word both ways, but you may not have a chance to get into a debate—even a friendly one—with a contest judge.

note / notice: If you want to be really spot on when you use the word *note*, try the word *notice* first. If *notice* fits, then that's probably what you should use. If you absolutely must use *note,* try *make a note* to keep the ire of sticklers from interfering with your career. I break this rule all the time, but not in a query letter or the first three chapters of a book that will be perused by an agent or editor. (See below for the correct use of the word *perused.*)

one in the same / one and the same: The words to use are *one and the same,* never *one in the same.*

palette / pallet / palate: These words are easy to distinguish when we see them all together, but they are sooo easy to overlook when we see them used incorrectly in our text. *Palette i*s the lovely little egg-shaped board with a hole cut out of it that painters use to mix their colors. *Palette* could also refer to a group of colors you intend to use when you redecorate your living room. A *pallet* is one of those wood carriers used to facilitate the shipping of a large number of small boxes, say your just-published book. *Palate* is that soft place in the back of your mouth, the place they once thought was the seat of your taste buds. That's why it's also used in context with tasting and food.

peddling / pedaling: Both are verbs. You'll need some kind of a foot-driven vehicle to do any *pedaling.* And something to sell to do any *peddling.*

peeked / peaked / piqued: The problem with these triplets is that they are not only frequently confused but that *piqued* is often pronounced *pee-kayd* (usually listed in dictionaries as a second choice or no choice at all) instead of *peeked.* Our interest may *peak* (if it reaches its highest point) but it more probably will be *piqued* (if something catches our interest or we are curious about something). *Peeked,* as you can see, is about *peering* or *glancing* and isn't related but sounds identical to the other two and sometimes our typing fingers just tap it into our copy.

peruse / browse: Many people are using *peruse* to mean checking something over quickly. It means quite the opposite, though the meaning may shift from the sheer weight of misuse. Use *peruse* when you mean to look at something closely. To avoid having an editor think you are wrong even when you have it right, you may want to avoid it altogether. With some words you just can't win.

picturesque / picaresque: *Picaresque* usually refers to a literary character who is an adventurous rogue of the *Tom Jones* (by Henry Fielding) variety. Even writers won't have occasion to use it often. *Picaresque* characters may also be *picturesque* (suited to pictures in a quaint or exceptionally beautiful way), but use the spelling that best suits your meaning. By the way— to be gender fair here—Daniel Defoe's *Moll Flanders* is also *picaresque.*

pier / peer: I had this wrong in the title of a poem I was presenting in class once. Quite embarrassing. My word processor offered no red alert. I was left to stew in my own lack of careful editing when I titled a poem "Death by Ferris Wheel at Santa Monica Peer." I don't have to tell you how much I wished I'd had a second pair of eyes look at my printed copies before I passed them to my fellows. This experience gives me a chance to remind you to be forgiving of others when they error; your turn is sure to come.

podium / lectern: These two are often confused in speech and that makes it doubly difficult for a writer or editor to spot. The *lectern* is the tall stand that speakers stand behind. It often has a mic attached and a ledge to hold books or notes. Some- times—but not always—it stands on a *podium*, a kind of riser used by conductors. Merriam-Webster lists *podium* as a second choice because it is used interchangeably with *lectern* so frequently, but we're after zero-tolerance in our writing.

proscribe / prescribe: *Proscribe* is to banish or prohibit. *Prescribe* is to establish a guideline or rule which is what doctors do when they write a prescription for you.

rap / wrap: Because both of these words are used colloquially and not very often, it is easy to get into the typing mode and use them incorrectly. Among other things, *rap* is slang used by law enforcement for a criminal charge. Among other familiar uses, *wrap* is used in the film industry when something is done, as in "It's a *wrap*." And what about when *rap* is used to describe a kind of improvised street music that rhymes? They aren't hard to tell apart, just easy to miss.

regards / in regards: It's never *in regards*. *Regards* is the plural of *regard*. We would say "in reference to," not "In references to." Having said that, *regards* is sometimes used as a formal substitute for phrases like "Say 'hi' for me!" and also means a kind of honoring. Perhaps it is most famously used as a lyric and song title by George M. Cohan: "Give my regards to Broadway."

rite / right / write: You don't need definitions of these words because they are not troublesome until we put them into commonly used phrases, like "rite of passage." *Rite*, please. Not *right*—or for that matter—*write*.

raze / raise: These words mean exactly the opposite. You know that *raise* means to build or grow something or to elevate something. *To raze* is to tear something down completely, to level it to the ground. Let's *raise* our glasses to toast our confusing English language.

to rise / to raise: Here we have verbs similar to *to lie* and *to lay*. *To raise* requires a direct object. *To rise* doesn't. We *raise* the blind in the morning. The sun *rises* in the morning.

repel / repulse: Both words are used to mean approximately the same thing. *Repulse* is stronger, though. When you use one, consciously choose whichever is more accurate.

restive / restless: *Restive* is more about describing an action or situation in which someone is being unresponsive than is the word *restless*. Politicians often react *restively* and then wonder why they must confront a *restless* or hostile crowd.

setup / set up: Oh, words that can be pushed together can be headaches. *Setup* is a noun and refers to an arrangement. In a crime story, the protagonist might say, "Here's the *setup*." Sometimes *setup* is used by cooks and others to refer to the organization of their ingredients and tools. *Set up* (two words) is a verb. "We set up the chairs around the tables." It requires a direct object.

simple / simplistic: These words are not interchangeable. *Simple* is *un*complicated. *Simplistic* is oversimplified—usually to a fault. Occasionally we hear *simple* used to mean oversimplified as we do in the nursery rhyme "Simple Simon." In the poem, Simon has limited understanding. Using the word this way is not only antiquated, it is not politically correct.

sight / site / cite: *Sight* refers to vision as a noun but also as a verb. *Site* refers to a location. *Cite* is a verb meaning to refer to something like a resource, as in research. It is related to the noun *citation* when it means to give a ticket.

social / sociable: Many use *social* when they mean *sociable*. People may be friendly or *sociable*; i.e., they may exhibit sociable behavior. A connection with another is *social*, a *social* club or a *social* ranking.

solve / resolve: Use *solve* as a verb to mean figuring something out. *Resolve* is a noun for committing to an action or idea. "He was *resolved* not to make a single error in his essay." "Her *resolve* was impressive."

swum: Just know that, as odd as it sounds, *swum* is a word and it takes a helping verb. "He has *swum* many races in his day."

strive / strove / have striven: This is a hotly contested verb in style and grammar books. Yes, you may pass the critical eye of many editors if you use *strived* in the simple past—the *Wall Street Journal* used it often enough (once?) for Garner's editors to wag their fingers at them—but we're after zero tolerance here. You'll want to stick with the most frequently accepted declination of this verb: *strive / strove / striven.* Write "Yesterday I *strove* to be a better grammarian; today I'm not so sure about my effort," if you want to be first-choice perfect.

tack / tact: These are very different words but because they sound similar, people often type them wrong. *Tact* is the ability not to offend someone. *To tack* is to swerve or move in a zig-zagging way. Of course, it's also a little flat-headed nail-like thing we use to post papers on bulletin boards or for the process of putting things together in carpentry.

teem / team: *Teem* is to swarm or have an abundance of. "The river is *teeming* with fish." A *team* is a group of people brought together to perform a function.

throws / throes: You know the difference, but I'll bet you type *throws* on the rare occasion you want to say *throes.* "When I am in the *throes* of writing, I rarely eat." If the words do confuse you, keep in mind that *throws* is a verb.

tide you over / tie you over: When we're children, we are uninformed because our knowledge is limited. If we never see the same phrase in print, we continue to make the error (or if we do, we pay no attention). *Tide* is correct here, not *tie.*

tort / torte: *Tort* is a legal term, a wrong or harm done other than by a breach of contract. *Torte* comes from Latin. It was a kind of twisted cake in the days of the Romans and still means *cake* though it needn't be twisted these days.

tough row to hoe / tough road to hoe: In phrases like this, try to think of how the phrase might have originated. This is term that comes from gardening or farming; a *hoe* is a tool used for weeding or making furrows. So it's a tough *row*. If one thinks about it, one would rarely have an occasion to *hoe* a road.

urban / urbane: *Urban* means related to or located in a city. *Urbane* means refined and elegant or, as some might say, "citified."

use / utilize: There is nothing wrong with either word, but don't use *utilize* when plain old *use* will suffice. In a query letter it sounds sooooo stuffy to say, "I would utilize my skills as a publicist to market (your title here)." Use *utilize* in a more technical sense, that is, when you want to make use of something or find a practical use for something. "This faucet *utilizes* a new filtering technology." Even then, as you can see, you could conceivably choose *uses* and sound less officious.

verbage / verbiage: There is no such word as *verbage*. What you are after is *verbiage* and it means the manner in which something is expressed verbally.

veil / vale: Most of us know the difference here. *Veil* is something sheer (either material or figurative) that helps obscure something. *Vale* is a rather antiquated word for a small valley. When we put the word into a clichéd phrase like "vale of tears," we may not even think of *vale* because we rarely use the word except in another clichéd phrase, "over hill and *vale*." Come to think of it, the cliché I was looking for was probably "over hill and *dale*." See how dangerous those oft-repeated phrases are?

waiver / waver: *Waiver* is the noun often used in official situations that means to put aside or give reprieve to something. *Waver* means to tremble or sway. People are using the word *waffle* now instead of *waver*, perhaps because they aren't sure of how to use *waver*.

wile / while: These two rarely get misused because the writer doesn't know the difference. Rather the writer mistypes and then may not notice the error. Spell Checker sure isn't going to help. When *while* is used as verb it means to spend time idly. So we say, "*while* away the hours." *Wile* is a verb that means to entice or a noun (usually used in the plural) or an adjective to describe a deceitful character trait. Thus we have that cartoon character, Wile E. Coyote.

wreak / reek: *Wreak* means to inflict. *Reek* means to stink. So we write "to *wreak* havoc" even when we believe the havoc we *wreaked* has caused a rather smelly situation.

Reading: One Editing Book at a Time

This list expands the superb (seriously!) list of the editing-related books in the appendices the second edition of my book, *The Frugal Editor: Put Your Best Book Forward to Avoid Humiliation and Ensure Success*. http://bit.ly/FrugalEditor

Joy of Syntax: A Simple Guide to All the Grammar Rules You Should Know by June Casagrande, Ten Speed Press. http://bit.ly/JoyofSyntax

The Elements of Style: Fourth Edition, William Strunk and E.B. White, Pearson. I'm giving you a half-hearted recommendation, here, and I suspect this will surprise you. This book is best for academics or those trying to manage English as a second language. English is no longer as rule-oriented or as static as people think it is and this book—though it still uses the word *style* in the title—may suffer from its fifty years of being misused or misunderstood. If you choose to study it, don't use the copy of an earlier edition you may have on your bookshelf. Insist on the Fourth Edition because it's better at making "style" clearer. Find it at http://bit.ly/StyleChoices.

The Birds and Bees of Words: A Guide to the Most Common Errors in Usage, Spelling, and Grammar by Mary Embree, Allworth Press. http://bit.ly/BirdsBeesGram

The Author's Toolkit: A Step-By-Step Guide to Writing a Book by Mary Embree, Seaview Publishing, a Writer's Digest Book Club selection. http://bit.ly/ToolkitbyEmbree

Just So You Know: Before You Publish

How to Publish and Promote Your Book Now by L. Diane Wolfe. Dancing Lemur Press. A Kindle edition at only 99 cents. http://bit.ly/DianeWolfe

10 Publishing Myths by W. Terry Whalin might be the best go-to book for any writer considering publishing of any kind. Morgan James Publishing. http://bit.ly/TerrysMyths

Other Writers' Tools from Carolyn Howard-Johnson

- The Frugal Book Promoter, 3rd Edition
- The Frugal Editor
- How to Get Great Book Reviews Frugally and Ethically
- The Great First Impression Book Proposal, 2nd Edition
- Great Little Last-Minute Editing Tips for Writers (you're reading it this very minute!)

**Watch for the latest special deals on my books at
ModernHistoryPress.com/frugal
Use Coupon Code "GOFRUGAL" for best savings!**

Unsolicited Praise for Carolyn's HowToDoItFrugally Series

"… I want to tell you how remarkably useful and efficient your HowToDoItFrugally Series is… I just joined AuthorsDen, posted various things in all the little boxes. Ms. Ho-Jo, you rock! Millions of thanks for the care and effort you have invested, and for your fabulous sense of organization. My media kit is all set up and being filled in. Whew!"

~Deborah Hicks Midanek (Bailey),
author of *The Governance Revolution*

The Frugal Book Promoter:
How to get nearly free publicity on your
own or partnering with your publisher
3rd Edition

This multi award-winner, now in its third edition, has been Carolyn's HowToDoIt-Frugally Series flagship book for going on two decades. For only a few cents a day, *The Frugal Book Promoter* assures your book the best possible start in life. The author was inspired to write this book full of nitty-gritty how-tos for getting nearly-free publicity for her UCLA Writers' Program class. A former publicist, journalist, and retailer, Carolyn shares her professional experience as well as practical tips gleaned from the successes of her own book campaigns. She tells authors how to do what their publishers can't or won't and why authors can often do their own promotion better than a PR professional.

~ ~ ~

"If one were to look up and read all the advice writers are offered herein, one would deserve a Master's in promoting and marketing, at the least."

~ Tupelo Review

"This newly updated third edition of *The Frugal Book Promoter* assures even the most novice of authors get their book the best possible start in life. That's true whether their publisher assigns zero dollars or thousands to their book's marketing campaign. Carolyn is a former publicist who draws upon her years of experience to give authors the no-nonsense basics required to build a time-saving social media campaign and knock 'em dead lists of influencers that will be more effective than anything paid advertising could buy. Authors can pick and choose from dozens of ideas for promotions that Carolyn developed or refined. There are campaign ideas, techniques and strategies to match any pocketbook and personality considerations."

~ Jim Cox, Midwest Book Review

"At last—a solid, sensible, systematic guide to the ins and outs of promotion and publicity...Carolyn Howard-Johnson proves that she's not only an accomplished poet, essayist, and novelist, but also a marketing maestro!"

~ JayCe Crawford, *Cup of Comfort* author, copyright professional

"...until now I didn't have many other staples to recommend to new authors looking for publicity."

~ Jenna Glatzer, author of *Make a Real Living as a Freelance Author*

"...chock full of ideas that even seasoned book promoters will not have tried...."

~ Dallas Hodder Franklin, writer

"*The Frugal Book Promoter*! I love it. Most authors don't have deep pockets for publicity, promotion, and marketing. The chapter on perks offered by Amazon is a perfect example of the kind of practical advice offered—the kind that took me months to discover."

~ Rolf Gompertz, author, veteran publicist for NBC, and UCLA instructor

"Carolyn Howard-Johnson started me on this whole journey of book publishing with her book *The Frugal Book Promoter*. I've hit best-seller status on Amazon several times since. I'm forever grateful to her."

~ Christopher Meeks, author and writing instructor at USC and other colleges

Awards across editions: Winner *USA Book News*, coveted *Irwin Award*, silver medal from *Military Writers Society of America*, honored by *Global Ebook Awards*

To order hardcover or paperback direct from the publisher and save 20%, please visit https://ModernHistoryPress.com/frugal and enter coupon code "GOFRUGAL" during checkout.

ISBN: 978-1-61599-468-7

Modern History Press

The Frugal Editor: Put Your Best Book Forward to Avoid Humiliation and Ensure Success, 2nd Edition
Subtitle: Do-it-yourself editing secrets for authors: From your query letter to final manuscript to the marketing of your new bestseller

> "Language is a fluid lifeform. To assume that because we once learned grammar one way, that way will always be accepted is fallacious. To neglect researching the language we write in when we so assiduously research the facts for what we write is folly." ~ Quote from *The Frugal Editor*

There are gremlins out there determined to keep your work from being published, your book from being promoted. Resolved to embarrass you before the gatekeepers who can turn the key of success for you, they lurk in your subconscious and the depths of your computer programs. Whether you are a new or experienced author, *The Frugal Editor* will help you present whistle-clean copy (from a one-page cover letter to your entire manuscript) to those who have the power to say "yea" or "nay."

"Using the basic computer and editing tricks from *The Frugal Editor*, authors can prevent headaches and save themselves time—and even money—during the editing process. It's well worth your effort to learn them."
~ Barbara McNichol, *Barbara McNichol Editorial*

Awards: Winner *USA Book News, Reader Views* Literary Award, Next Generation Marketing Award. The eBook is a Next Generation Indie Book Award finalist and was given an Honorable Mention by Dan Poynter's Global eBook Award.

Order this book as an eBook or paper on Amazon.

How to Get Great Book Reviews Frugally and Ethically
Subtitle: The ins and outs of using free reviews to build and sustain a writing career

How to Get Great Book Reviews Frugally and Ethically is the culmination of nearly two decades Carolyn Howard-Johnson spent helping writers avoid pitfalls, misconceptions, and out-and-out scams perpetrated on unsuspecting authors…and helping them reach their dreams of great reviews, great book tours, and great launches. It turns out that *How to Get Great Book Reviews* is the essence for a successful marketing campaign that includes all those things and—more importantly—for building the readership necessary for a prosperous writing career.

"The most comprehensive book on getting book reviews I've ever come across. In her usual warm and easy-to-follow manner, Howard-Johnson outlines everything you need to know to maximize your book's chances…an excellent resource that both beginning and seasoned authors can return to again and again" ~ Magdalena Ball, owner of the prestigious review site, CompulsiveReader.com

Available on Amazon in paper or as an e-book.

ISBN-13: 978-1536948370

Reference Guides in the Multi Award-Winning HowToDoItFrugally Series of Books for Writers

The Great First Impression Book Proposal Subtitle: Everything You Need to Know To Sell Your Book in Thirty Minutes or Less 2nd Edition

This booklet, now in its second edition, is the result of multi award-winning author Carolyn Howard-Johnson's extensive work with clients who hate writing book proposals and hate *learning* how to write them even more. She found herself coaching them through the process rather than doing it for them, for who could possibly recreate the passion an author feels for his or her own book better than the author? In doing so, she found she had written a booklet—not a tome—that took her clients only about thirty minutes to absorb. Voila! *The Great First Impression Book Proposal* was born. WinningWriters.com offered it as an aid to the participants for their prestigious North Street Book Prize.

"Book Proposal" is the perfect career-boosting experience for those who want to learn how to wow an editor in no time flat with very little out-of-pocket and thirty minutes out of a busy schedule.

"I just finished reading *The Great First Impression Book Proposal*. I like your style and encouragement. I was a bit intimidated about finishing my book proposal. I was thinking it had to be stiff and boring. I even have dialogue in it. I thought I'd have to cut it out. Now, I'll probably leave it in."

~ Wanza Leftwich, author, blogger

"I love [*Great First Impression BookProposal*]! My husband was amazed at all the info crammed into this short book. You could have charged a lot more. I just re-vamped my proposal to follow the guidelines in it for my latest book."

~ Myrna Lou, palmist, psychic, and author

"Howard-Johnson writes with the experience of a professional and the candor of a best friend who doesn't want you to fall on your face. With humor and friendliness, she offers solid, practical tips. She is one of my favorite authors, and her books always top my must-have list. This one is no exception. It'll stay on my resource shelf. If you've ever thought about being an author, you need *The Great First Impression Book Proposal* in your resources."
~ Jennifer Akers, author, reviewer for MyShelf, and social media marketing expert

"...concise yet informative instruction manual on how to write a book proposal, author Carolyn Howard-Johnson offers a long list of golden-nugget-TO-DOs and smart ideas which can help guide writers past the Gatekeepers."
~ Kathe Gogolewski, author and artist

"Marketing is never easy... Well, it might be if you follow the easy steps CarolynHoward-Johnson offers up in *The Great First Impression Book Proposal: Everything You Need to Know About Selling Your Book in Thirty Minutes or Less*. Howard-Johnson's bulleted lists are superior. They are easy to understand, easy to implement, and even easier to read. She means it when she says thirty minutes or less. I will recommend this book to all of our authors and potential authors."
~ Georgia Jones, Editor-in-Chief, Ladybug Press and New Voices, Inc

"The creation of an effective book proposal cannot be over-emphasized as a basic skill set for all aspiring authors seeking publication of their work—and Carolyn Howard-Johnson is a time-tested expert on the subject. Every aspiring (and even seasoned) author needs to obtain and carefully read *The Great First Impression Book Proposal*—and every Creative Writing class should list *The Great First Impression Book Proposal* on their supplemental studies reading lists."
~ Jim Cox, *Midwest Book Review*

"When I first reviewed Carolyn Howard-Johnson's small book, little did I realize how dog-eared my paperback copy would get over time. I've been through it and book-marked it so many times that it's tattered beyond belief, but I cannot get rid of it. It appears that Ms. Howard-Johnson has also released it in an updated edition, and that's why my review predates this one. And please note that now *The Great First Impression Book Proposal* is available as a Kindle edition. As a Prime member I could have borrowed it for free, but since I know already how many highlights there will be, it was worth buying again in the Kindle edition. If you're an aspiring writer in any genre, it's well worth it."

~ John Williamson, *Amazon Top 1000 Vine Reviewer*

Available as hardcover, paperback, or ebook at ModernHistoryPress.com/frugal. Use the coupon code GOFRUGAL to get the special offer.

ISBN-13: 978-1-61599-481-6

Modern History Press

Blogs

Carolyn blogs at *Sharing with Writers and Readers* about everything from the marketing of books to what's new in the publishing world, plus writing prompts, and writing skills for both fiction and nonfiction. SharingwithWriters.blogspot.com.

The New Book Review is a blog where authors and reviewers recycle their favorite reviews for free. Follow the submission guidelines in the left column of the blog's home page or in a tab at the top of that page. TheNewBookReview.blogspot.com

The Frugal, Smart and Tuned-In Editor, a blog where you get your editing questions answered so you can shop your book to the best agents and publishers with confidence. It helps self publishers turn out a more professional product, too. Please visit: TheFrugalEditor.blogspot.com

Visit Carolyn's website at https://howtodoitfrugally.com

> Careers that are not fed die as readily as any living organism given no sustenance.

About the Author

Carolyn Howard-Johnson brings her
experience as a publicist, journalist,
marketer, editor, and retailer to the
advice she gives in her HowToDo-
ItFrugally Series of books for writers
and the many classes she taught for
nearly a decade as instructor for
UCLA Extension's world-renown
Writers' Program including a class on
editing for self-publishers. The books
in her HowToDoItFrugally Series of
books for writers have won multiple
awards. That series includes *The
Frugal Book Promoter* and *The
Frugal Editor* which won awards from *USA Book News*, *Reader
Views* Literary Award, the marketing award from Next
Generation Indie Books and others including the coveted Irwin
award. *How to Get Great Book Reviews Frugally and
Ethically* launched to rave reviews from Karen Cioffi, *The Article
Writing Doctor*:

> "I'm an author, content writer, and online marketing
> instructor. Reading Carolyn Howard-Johnson's *The
> Frugal Editor* has given me lots and lots of tips and
> reminders on how to write right, whether I'm writing
> fiction, nonfiction, blogging, or marketing. It's a writing
> tool I'll refer to over and over again."

Howard-Johnson is the recipient of the California Legislature's
Woman of the Year in Arts and Entertainment Award, and her
community's Character and Ethics award for her work promoting
tolerance with her writing. She was also named to *Pasadena
Weekly's* list of "Fourteen San Gabriel Valley women who make

life happen" and was given her community's Diamond Award for Achievement in the Arts.

The author loves to travel. She has visited nearly 100 countries and has studied writing at Cambridge University in the United Kingdom; Herzen University in St. Petersburg, Russia; and Charles University, Prague. She has been in love with words and syntax since she took an advanced grammar class from Miss Jones (no kidding!) in high school and, curiously followed up with grammar from a professor who was of Russian royalty at USC and another in Heiroglyphics from a professor who was made a Duke for his service during the great flood of Florence in 1966. Carolyn's website is www.howtodoitfrugally.com.

Index